EXPLORING COUNTRIES

Iraq

by Lisa Owings

BLASTOFF!
5
READERS

BELLWETHER MEDIA • MINNEAPOLIS, MN

Note to Librarians, Teachers, and Parents:

Blastoff! Readers are carefully developed by literacy experts and combine standards-based content with developmentally appropriate text.

Level 1 provides the most support through repetition of high-frequency words, light text, predictable sentence patterns, and strong visual support.

Level 2 offers early readers a bit more challenge through varied simple sentences, increased text load, and less repetition of high-frequency words.

Level 3 advances early-fluent readers toward fluency through increased text and concept load, less reliance on visuals, longer sentences, and more literary language.

Level 4 builds reading stamina by providing more text per page, increased use of punctuation, greater variation in sentence patterns, and increasingly challenging vocabulary.

Level 5 encourages children to move from "learning to read" to "reading to learn" by providing even more text, varied writing styles, and less familiar topics.

Whichever book is right for your reader, Blastoff! Readers are the perfect books to build confidence and encourage a love of reading that will last a lifetime!

This edition first published in 2011 by Bellwether Media, Inc.

No part of this publication may be reproduced in whole or in part without written permission of the publisher. For information regarding permission, write to Bellwether Media, Inc., Attention: Permissions Department, 5357 Penn Avenue South, Minneapolis, MN 55419.

Library of Congress Cataloging-in-Publication Data
Owings, Lisa.
 Iraq / by Lisa Owings.
  p. cm. – (Exploring countries) (Blastoff! readers)
Includes bibliographical references and index.
Summary: "Developed by literacy experts for students in grades three through seven, this book introduces young readers to the geography and culture of Iraq"–Provided by publisher.
ISBN 978-1-60014-592-6 (hardcover : alk. paper)
1. Iraq–Juvenile literature. I. Title.
DS70.62.O85 2011
956.7–dc22   2010039205

Printed in the United States of America, North Mankato, MN.

010111   1176

Contents

Where Is Iraq?   4

The Land   6

The Mesopotamian Marshes   8

Wildlife   10

The People   12

Daily Life   14

Going to School   16

Working   18

Playing   20

Food   22

Holidays   24

Iraqi Monuments   26

Fast Facts   28

Glossary   30

To Learn More   31

Index   32

Turkey

Iran

Tigris

Syria

Euphrates

Baghdad

Jordan

Iraq

Saudi Arabia

Did you know?

The Tigris and Euphrates river valleys were home to the Sumerian civilization, one of the oldest in history. The Sumerians lived in the area almost 6,000 years ago!

4

Shatt al-Arab

Kuwait

Persian Gulf

Iraq is a small country in the **Middle East**. Stretching across 169,235 square miles (438,317 square kilometers), it is surrounded by six other countries. Turkey lies to the north, Syria and Jordan to the west, and Saudi Arabia to the south. Iraq shares its entire eastern border with Iran. It has a short southeastern border with Kuwait.

Two major rivers, the Tigris and the Euphrates, flow across Iraq. They join to form the Shatt al-Arab, a river that empties into the Persian **Gulf**. Baghdad, the capital of Iraq, sits on the banks of the Tigris River.

Iraq is mostly a dry, flat country. The Tigris and the Euphrates rivers divide it into three parts. Southwest of the Euphrates lies a large desert region. This area includes the Syrian Desert. The land between the rivers is called Mesopotamia. Upper Mesopotamia is hilly and dry. A number of **salt flats** can be found there. Lower Mesopotamia has **fertile** plains and marshes. Northeast of the Tigris, the land rises into the high peaks of the Zagros Mountains. These run along Iraq's borders with Turkey and Iran.

fun fact

Sandstorms and dust storms are common during dry Iraqi summers. Strong winds lift the sand and dust into clouds as tall as 5,000 feet (1,524 meters)!

Did you know?

Iraqi summers are very hot. Temperatures average around 90 degrees Fahrenheit (32 degrees Celsius). Winters are mild, but snow often falls in the mountains.

The Mesopotamian Marshes surround the area where the Tigris and Euphrates rivers join. This is the largest area of **wetlands** in the Middle East. The Mesopotamian Marshes are green with tall reeds. The Ma'dan people, or Marsh Arabs, have lived in these marshes for thousands of years.

In the 1990s, Iraqi president Saddam Hussein drained the Mesopotamian Marshes. Most of the Ma'dan lost their homes and had to change their way of life. Today, close to half of the marshlands have been flooded again. Some Ma'dan have returned to their traditional homes. They still fish, grow rice, and raise water buffalo as their **ancestors** did.

Did you know?

The Ma'dan use reeds to make canoe-like boats, which they use to move through the marshes. They also make their homes from lightweight reeds because marshland is too wet to hold heavy buildings.

sacred ibis

Did you know?

Now that the marshes are being restored, rare birds like the Basra reed warbler and the sacred ibis are beginning to return to Iraq.

Iraq's varied landscape is home to many animals. Lizards, snakes, and other desert animals come out at night when it is cool. Rodents like the jerboa scurry across the sand to find food and water. Wild pigs and water buffalo flourish in the marshes. In the forests, the striped hyena and the Eurasian lynx stalk their prey.

jerboa

striped hyena

locust

Around 400 kinds of birds can be found in Iraq. Sandgrouses live in the deserts and plains. Herons wade in the rivers and marshes as kingfishers swoop overhead. Hawks, eagles, and owls hunt for prey throughout the country.

fun fact

Iraq has a very young population. Four out of every ten Iraqis are 14 years old or younger.

Iraq is home to over 29 million people. About three out of every four Iraqis are Arabs. Small numbers of Turkmen, Assyrians, and Armenians also live in Iraq. Many of these groups have been living in and around Iraq for thousands of years.

Kurds live in the northeast, in a region called Iraqi Kurdistan. About one out of every six Iraqis is Kurdish. The Kurds have their own government and way of life. Kurdish became an official language after Iraq wrote a new **constitution** in 2004. The other official language is Arabic, which is spoken by most Iraqis.

Speak Arabic!

Iraqis use Arabic script when they write. However, Arabic words can be written in English to help you say them out loud.

English	Iraqi Arabic	How to say it
hello	marhaba	MAR-hah-bah
good-bye	ma'a s-salaama	mah-as sah-LE-mah
yes	na'am	nahm
no	laa	lah
please	min fazlak	min FAHZ-lehk
thank you	shukran	SHU-krahn
friend	sadiiq	sah-DEEKH

fun fact

In Iraqi cities, people drive cars, ride buses, or walk to get from place to place. In the countryside, people use camels, donkeys and horses for transportation.

Though conditions are improving, daily life in Iraq has been greatly affected by war. Some areas still lack food, water, and electricity. Most Iraqis live in crowded apartments in cities. In the countryside, most people live in brick houses near rivers. Almost every city and village has an open-air market where people can shop for goods.

Religion is an important part of daily life in Iraq. Almost all Iraqis follow Islam. They pray five times a day. Both men and women wear long clothing to cover their bodies. Many women wear the traditional *hijab*, or head scarf.

Where People Live in Iraq

countryside 33%

cities 67%

Iraqi children start school at age 6 and continue until they are 12. They study Arabic, English, history, math, and science. If students want to move on to secondary school, they must pass a tough exam. Some students choose to go to a **vocational school** instead. Most Iraqis, however, go straight to work.

Students who graduate from secondary school can go to university. Many Iraqi students are now able to attend universities in other countries. They often study education, engineering, business, or medicine.

Did you know?
Decades of war have damaged Iraq's education system. Many people are working to repair school buildings, train new teachers, and provide students with new textbooks.

17

Working

Iraq is one of the world's largest producers of dates. These fruits have been grown in the country for thousands of years. Today, over ten million date trees can be found in Iraq.

Where People Work in Iraq

services 60%

manufacturing 19%

farming 21%

Most people in Iraq's countryside are oil workers, farmers, or fishermen. Oil workers drill into the earth to bring oil up from underground. They **refine** it into gasoline and other products. Farmers grow wheat, rice, vegetables, and dates. Some tend flocks of sheep. Iraqi fishermen bring in catches of carp and catfish from the rivers and lakes.

In cities, many Iraqis have **service jobs**. They work in banks, hospitals, schools, restaurants, and stores. Factory workers produce **textiles**, cement, and chemicals. Construction workers are busy trying to rebuild Iraq after many years of war.

Most Iraqis enjoy playing and watching sports. Their favorite sport is soccer. Thousands of people gather at the Al Shaab stadium to watch the national soccer team play. Others watch the games on television. Volleyball, weight lifting, and pigeon racing are other popular sports.

Iraqis also love to spend time with family and friends. They enjoy talking over coffee or going to see movies, plays, and concerts. Families often visit the Baghdad Zoo or the National Museum of Iraq. Holy sites in cities like Samarra, Karbala, and Al-Najaf attract people from all over the country.

! fun fact

In pigeon racing, handlers release trained pigeons from a faraway place and time how long it takes them to fly home. The trainer of the fastest bird wins!

Iraqi families gather together for almost every meal. They start the day with a light breakfast of bread with fruit or cheese. Many Iraqis also enjoy yogurt and eggs in the morning. Lunch is the main meal of the day, and dinner is often leftovers from lunch. For these meals, chicken or lamb is coated in spices and grilled. Flatbread, rice, and vegetables are always served with the main dish.

Masgouf is prepared for special events. This is Iraq's national dish. It is made with carp from the Tigris River. A fish is sliced open with the skin still on it, then sprinkled with salt and cooked over an open fire. For dessert, dates are often enjoyed with thick black coffee.

masgouf

Did you know?

Baklava and *kleicha* are popular desserts in Iraq. *Baklava* is a pastry layered with nuts and honey. *Kleicha* are traditional cookies filled with dates or nuts.

baklava

Most holidays in Iraq are Islamic holidays. **Ramadan** is one of the most important. It lasts for one month, during which Muslims **fast** from sunrise to sunset. Eid al-Fitr is a three-day celebration that marks the end of Ramadan. Muslims feast, pray, and exchange gifts.

Many Iraqi holidays honor the country's history. October 3 is National Day. It marks Iraq's independence from the United Kingdom in 1932. Iraqis also celebrate the day their country became a **republic**. Every year on July 14, they gather in the streets for Republic Day. Liberation Day falls on April 9. This day celebrates freedom from Saddam Hussein's rule and remembers those who died to free their country.

Al-Shaheed Monument

Iraq has many monuments that are important to its people. The half-domes of the Al-Shaheed Monument tower 131 feet (40 meters) over Baghdad. It was built to honor Iraqi soldiers. The Monument to the Unknown Soldier is another war **memorial**. It is shaped like a giant shield. A spiral-shaped structure next to the shield looks like a snail shell. It represents the **Minaret** of Samarra.

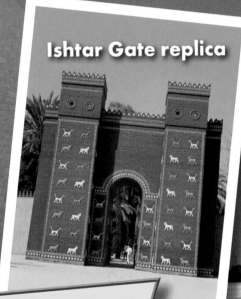

Ishtar Gate replica

fun fact

The original Ishtar Gate can be seen in the Pergamon Museum in Berlin, Germany.

The Ishtar Gate once stood at the entrance to the historic city of Babylon. Iraqis later built a **replica** of the gate. All of these monuments represent Iraq's rich history and its past and present struggles for peace.

Fast Facts About Iraq

الله اكبر

Iraq's Flag

The current Iraqi flag has three horizontal stripes. The top stripe is red, the center is white, and the bottom is black. The green Arabic script in the center of the white stripe means "God is great." The colors represent sacrifice, fertile fields, battle, and purity. This version of the Iraqi flag was adopted in 2008. The flag may change in the future to better represent the new Iraq.

Official Name: Republic of Iraq

Area: 169,235 square miles (438,317 square kilometers); Iraq is the 58th largest country in the world.

Capital City:	Baghdad
Important Cities:	Basra, Mosul, Kirkuk, Arbil
Population:	29,671,605 (July 2010)
Official Languages:	Arabic and Kurdish
National Holidays:	Republic Day (July 14), Liberation Day (April 9), National Day (October 3)
Religions:	Muslim (97%), Other (3%)
Major Industries:	farming, fishing, manufacturing, mining, services
Natural Resources:	oil, natural gas, phosphates
Manufactured Products:	chemicals, clothing, construction materials, metals, food products
Farm Products:	wheat, barley, rice, vegetables, dates, cotton, cattle, sheep, poultry
Unit of Money:	dinar

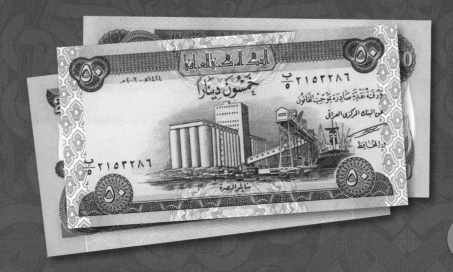

Glossary

ancestors—relatives who lived long ago

constitution—the basic principles and laws of a nation

fast—to choose not to eat

fertile—supports growth

gulf—part of an ocean or sea that extends into land

memorial—a structure built to honor and remember people or an event

Middle East—a region in northeastern Africa and southwestern Asia

minaret—a tower next to a mosque; people stand in minarets to call Muslims to prayer.

Ramadan—the ninth month of the Islamic calendar; Ramadan is a time when Muslims fast from sunrise to sunset.

refine—to remove unwanted parts of a material; Iraqi oil workers refine oil to make gasoline and other products.

replica—a copy of an original

republic—a nation governed by elected leaders instead of a monarch

salt flats—salt-covered areas of land

service jobs—jobs that perform tasks for people or businesses

textiles—fabrics or clothes that have been woven or knitted

vocational school—a school that trains students to do specific jobs

wetlands—wet, spongy lands; bogs, marshes, and swamps are wetlands.

To Learn More

AT THE LIBRARY

Augustin, Byron, and Jake Kubena. *Iraq*. New York, N.Y.: Children's Press, 2006.

Samuels, Charlie. *Iraq*. Washington, D.C.: National Geographic, 2007.

Taus-Bolstad, Stacy. *Iraq in Pictures*. Minneapolis, Minn.: Lerner Publications, 2004.

ON THE WEB

Learning more about Iraq is as easy as 1, 2, 3.

1. Go to www.factsurfer.com.

2. Enter "Iraq" into the search box.

3. Click the "Surf" button and you will see a list of related Web sites.

With factsurfer.com, finding more information is just a click away.

Index

activities, 21
Baghdad, 4, 5, 26
capital (see Baghdad)
daily life, 14-15
education, 16-17
Eid al-Adha, 24
Eid al-Fitr, 24
Euphrates River, 4, 5, 6, 8
food, 22-23
holidays, 24-25
housing, 9, 14
Islam, 15, 24
landscape, 6-9
language, 13, 16
Liberation Day, 25
location, 4-5
Mesopotamian Marshes, 8-9, 10
Middle East, 5, 8
monuments, 26-27
National Day, 25
peoples, 8-9, 12-13
Ramadan, 24
Republic Day, 25
Saddam Hussein, 9, 25
Shatt al-Arab River, 5
sports, 20
Tigris River, 4, 5, 6, 8
transportation, 9, 14

war, 14, 17, 26
wildlife, 10-11
working, 18-19

The images in this book are reproduced through the courtesy of: Jane Sweeney / Age Fotostock, front cover, pp. 26-27; Maisei Raman, front cover (flag), p. 28; Yahya Epparlama, pp. 4-5; Department of Defense, p. 6 (small); dbimages / Alamy, pp. 6-7; V Theakston / Age Fotostock, p. 8; Tina Manley / Asia / Alamy, p. 9; Panoramic Images / Getty Images, pp. 10-11; Juniors Bildarchiv / Alamy, p. 11 (top); Juan Martinez, pp. 11 (middle & bottom), 29 (bill); Jane Sweeney / Getty Images, p. 12; Targa Targa / Photolibrary, p. 14; MARKA / Alamy, p. 15; Shehzad Noorani / Photolibrary, p. 16; AFP / Getty Images, pp. 17, 20; Images & Stories / Alamy, pp. 18, 22, 24; David Bacon / Alamy, p. 19 (left); Nordicphotos / Alamy, p. 19 (right); Getty Images, p. 21; Eddie Gerald / Alamy, p. 23 (top); Murat Baysan, p. 23 (bottom); Wim Van Cappellen / Photolibrary, p. 25; Robert Harding Picture Library Ltd / Alamy, p. 27 (small).